THE JUMBO BOOK OF HIDDEN PICTURES

MORE THAN **1000** OBJECTS TO FIND!

Compiled by the Editors of

Highlights for Children

BOYDS MILLS PRESS

Cover:

Penguin Paradise

The penguins are vacationing at their favorite frozen resort. Hidden there are fifteen objects: Mr. Wind, a mushroom, flashlight, bag, flower basket, bird, fish, bowl, ladder, house, mitten, chef, baseball cap, goat's head, and jar. How many can you find?

Copyright © 1992 by Boyds Mills Press
Contents copyright © by Highlights for Children, Inc.
All rights reserved

Boyds Mills Press, Inc.
A Highlights Company
815 Church Street
Honesdale, Pennsylvania 18431
Printed in the United States of America

Publisher Cataloging-in-Publication Data
The jumbo book of hidden pictures / compiled by the editors of Highlights for Children.
[96]p. ; ill. ; cm.
Summary: Each page presents a challenge to find various objects within a picture.
ISBN 1-56397-021-X
1. Puzzles—Juvenile literature. [1. Picture puzzles.] I. Highlights for Children. II. Title.
793.73—dc20   [E]   1992
Library of Congress Catalog Card Number: 91-72975

First edition, 1992
Book designed by Cathryn Falwell

20 19 18

Marathon Race

As the children race, can you find the seventeen objects hiding on and around them? Look for a book, baton, bottle, pencil, garden hoe, bowl, hammer, earthworm, mug, horseshoe, candle, mouse, toothbrush, apple core, fishhook, slice of bread, and cat.

Sailing the Santa Maria

Christopher Columbus and his crew battle a vicious Atlantic storm. In this picture find the golf club, tweezers, clamp, pizza slice, trowel, spoon, fish, steering wheel, ice skate, bolt, sheep's head, wrench, plum, boot, necklace, dinghy, and telephone receiver.

Little Red Riding Hood

"My, what beautiful eyes you have, Red Riding Hood," says the wolf wearing Grandmother's clothing. In this picture find the fork, slice of bread, muffin, saltshaker, rose, piece of candy, celery, slice of cheese, jar, teabag, drinking straw, mug, drumstick, and piece of pie.

The Bagel, Pretzel Bakery

The elves are working very hard to make these tasty treats. Hiding in their bakery are twenty objects: a paintbrush, chef's hat, wizard, cane, can, elf shoe, cup, mop, friendly ghost, elf hat, saw, fish, book, gavel, dress, telescope, iron, baseball bat, pot, and toothbrush. Can you find them all?

Working in the Garden

The young twins are busy weeding and watering. In their garden portrait find the light bulb, wishbone, spoon, bell, paintbrush, pen, sandwich, baseball, glove, iron, ice-cream cone, rose, cupcake, flute, and cap.

Abe Lincoln Chopping Wood

When Abe Lincoln lived in a log cabin, one of his chores was chopping wood. While Abe works, can you find the eagle's head, feather, saw, fish, boomerang, bird, cat, coonskin cap, fork, hatchet, dog's head, sickle, book, frying pan, and turtle?

Loon's Nest

While the loon calls a warning, can you find the nine hidden objects? Look for the sheep, scissors, carrot, fly, umbrella, frog, spectacles, banana, and tweezers.

Paul Revere

"The British are coming!" Paul Revere cries to the colonists late one night. In this picture can you find the ship, lantern, rooster, dog, horseshoe, bell, numeral 1, pigeon, shoe, and anvil?

Grandpa's Bedtime Stories

All the children are happy when Grandpa reads a bedtime story. You, too, can have fun by finding the leaf, pear, iron, dog's head, pitcher, pliers, bow, mouse, light bulb, paintbrush, boomerang, sailboat, hammer, and envelope.

Downtown Main Street

It's a busy day in this booming metropolis. Can you find the twenty-one objects hidden in and around all the activity? Watch out for traffic as you look for the car, sailboat, comb, shovel, toothbrush, fishing pole, ruler, flashlight, sleeping baby, radio, open box, open wallet, hat, mug, ice-cream cone, boot, briefcase, drawing table, key, elephant, and brush.

The Fox and the Crow

As the fox thinks about how to get the cheese from the crow, can you find the eight hidden objects? Look for an owl, swan, hen, squirrel, fish, high-button shoe, man's profile, and elephant's head.

Bambi Learns to Walk

Bambi's mother watches carefully as Bambi learns to walk. Also watching are fifteen hidden objects. Can you find the cat, dog's head, cup, boot, lady's face, duck, owl, turtle, bird, fox, raccoon, butterfly, fish, mouse, and tulip?

Aladdin and the Wonderful Lamp

As Aladdin rubs the lamp a third time, a great gust of wind brings a genie before him. Aladdin's first wish is for you to find all of the objects hidden in this picture. The fifteen objects are a starfish, lizard, tennis ball, book, sock, dolphin, cheese, trowel, peanut, shoe, clothespin, squirrel, cat, rocket, and teddy bear.

First Aid

It looks as though Tommy is in trouble when Suzy and Bernice practice their first-aid skills. Maybe you can do better by finding the fourteen objects hidden in this picture: a sailboat, goose, shark, saltshaker, opened banana, whistle, snail, iron, apple, ax, paintbrush, spoon, milk carton, and pair of sunglasses.

The Foal and Duckling

The duckling quacks good-bye to the foal as its family waddles away. In this picture look for the carrot, toothbrush, hammer, lamb, juicer, pie, tent, bear cub, lantern, star, lizard, cowbell, swan, and cowboy hat.

Nighttime Adventure

As the moon shines through the window, Sally Duck snuggles beneath the covers with her favorite book, <u>Adventure Tales.</u> Can you find the objects hidden in this picture: a mouse, ladle, slice of pie, bell, crayon, telephone receiver, whale, snail, cup, bone, hammer, fork, screwdriver, and candy cane?

This Ole House

It's fun to clean and care for a house that belongs to you. While the children work, can you find a hot dog, lamp, acorn, king, butterfly, boot, gavel, fish, sailboat, candle, thimble, purse, comb, gas pump, bow, pepper mill, pencil, ladder, telephone receiver, hat, torch, bubble pipe, jar, and mitten?

Maple Sugaring

It's snowy and cold, and it's maple sugaring time! Can you find the banana, pair of pants, grapes, candle, bow, spool, iron, lemon, ladle, crow, fork, lizard, pencil, and feather?

Corncob City Elves

As the elves go about their corny business, can you find the seventeen hidden objects? Look for a sprinkling can, girl, basket, scarf, elf shoe, toy soldier, ladder, candle, shovel, string of beads, man, flower, lantern, palm tree, snowman, campfire, and table.

21

A Day at the Beach

"Hey, everybody, come on in! The water's great!" Dad is the first one to test the water. While the children play in the sand, can you find the thirteen hidden objects: a suntan-lotion bottle, hat, spade, star, sailboat, shell, pail, surfboard, sandal, bird, fishhook, flipper, and pair of spectacles?

Mrs. Turtle Makes a Shopping List

Mrs. Turtle makes plans to fill her nearly empty refrigerator. While she writes, can you find the sixteen hidden objects? Look for a pig, worm, sock, slice of bread, flag, tree, brush, candle, fish, cup, chick, pencil, bone, cane, tent, and pair of pants.

Down on the Farm

Maribelle loves the salty taste of Jerry's hand. On the farm are twenty-two hidden objects: a hat, pair of pliers, broom, jump rope, slipper, cat, horse, bird, dog, duck, cow, clothespin, pitcher, screwdriver, hoe, toothbrush, frog, key, piece of pie, hammer, mouse, and candle.

Dogs on Bicycles

It's a close race as the dogs round the final bend. In this exciting picture find the duck, shark, hammer, butterfly, sea gull, otter, wasp, stocking cap, eagle's head, penguin, alligator, feather, and elf's head.

Cat Concert

With a "Meeeee-oooooowwwww!" the feline soprano finishes another great cat concert. In this picture find the belt, baseball bat, seal, paintbrush, broom, scissors, paper clip, mouse, pencil, record, carrot, knife, mallet, toothbrush, ski boot, and lady's boot.

Thomas Edison

How could Thomas Edison concentrate in all this commotion? Hidden in his lab are seventeen objects: a tricycle, chisel, loon, beet, bison, beaver, mitten, golf club, flashlight, snow shovel, trolley car, cardinal's head, hummingbird, pair of binoculars, paint roller, electric drill, and floppy disk.

Jungle Gym Fun

There are many ways to have fun on a jungle gym! You can have fun by finding the fifteen objects hidden in this picture: a fish, boot, carrot, bell, gavel, key, broom, pair of scissors, pencil, sailboat, snail, bat, safety pin, apple, and rabbit.

Hiking Hares

When the hares go hiking, they really go prepared. All they're missing are the fourteen hidden objects in the picture. Can you find a mouse, boot, acorn, octopus, hoe, sock, diver, pie, boat, watermelon slice, funnel, bear, adhesive bandage, and dustpan?

The Bremen Town Musicians

"OK, Dog, you play the fiddle," the donkey says as the four musicians plan their parade. Can you find the nine objects hidden in this picture? Look for a snail, lizard, fish, alligator's head, ice skate, pair of scissors, banana, bird, and candle.

Good Witches Make Cookies

What do good witches put in their cookies? Try to imagine while you look for the sixteen objects hidden in this picture: a trowel, carrot, rabbit, leaf of clover, rolling pin, jockey's helmet, saw, book, penguin, goblet, football, sailboat, magnet, broom, slice of bread, and telephone receiver.

Inventive Elves

These merry elves have invented a wind machine. Join in the fun by finding the bowl, pot, candle, slipper, boot, pencil, lamppost, bell, hat, sock, seashell, man, pliers, woman, safety pin, wizard's head, sitting elf, ostrich, and glass bottle.

Animal Farmer's Market

Cows, sheep, pigs, and rabbits are busy buying good things to eat at the farmer's market. Hidden in this picture are a bugle, pencil, carrot, sailboat, acorn, spoon, toothbrush, feather, mouse, kite, shoe, cup and saucer, baseball, fish, hammer, boy's head, crayon, and hatchet.

Space

Mr. Johnson points out some constellations in this spectacular evening sky. Can you point out the twelve objects hidden in this picture? Look for a rose, pushpin, fish, screwdriver, brush, whistle, measuring cup, monkey's face, candle, canoe, paintbrush, and feather.

Chickadees' Winter Feast

The chickadees feast on birdseed and suet. Also outdoors on this cold, snowy day are fourteen hidden objects: an iron, teapot, paintbrush, mitten, oar, hanger, pie, archery bow, bottle, goose, trowel, woodchuck, rabbit, and flower.

The Amusement Park

Many children, young and old, ride the rides and nibble on cotton candy at the amusement park. In this picture find the umbrella, parking meter, kite, man, rocket, sailboat, sock, spider web, ladder, spoon, horseshoe, coin, pickle, flower, and letters W, X, and H. There are seventeen objects.

Free Kittens

"Free kittens! Get a playful and lovable kitten for free!" While you pick out your favorite kitten, find the carrot, book, mitten, exclamation point, mouse, butterfly, saucer, goldfish, slice of pie, sea gull, watermelon slice, locket, and banana.

Farm Life

Milk and eggs fly on the farm when the dog runs away with Annie's belt. Hidden in this picture are twenty-two objects: a fish, toothbrush, turtle, sheep, dove, bucket, carrot, rabbit's head, bull's head, candle, frog, pair of glasses, book, trowel, sailboat, sleeping rabbit, clothespin, mouse, cat, duck, heart, and dog.

Creative Bears

The bears love to paint and draw and make a mess. Can you find the fourteen hidden objects: a turret, pencil, ruler, pair of pants, jar, purse, house, shoe, clown, man's head, tube of paint, book, elephant's head, and gingerbread man?

Puppies, Puppies, Puppies

The puppies race to greet Ben after school. In the picture are fourteen hidden objects: a beet, bell, ice-cream cone, canoe, key, bird, flamingo, whistle, umbrella, spoon, pair of scissors, fish, rabbit, and nail. Can you find them all?

Dinosaurs

During the Mesozoic era, dinosaurs roamed over our earth. In this picture are fourteen hidden objects: a mouse, stocking cap, car, parrot, bell, book, rooster's head, airplane, bathrobe, telephone receiver, roller skate, Pilgrim's hat, hamburger, and bugle.

41

Beavers Swimming

It's a day at the beach for these fun-loving beavers. In this picture can you find the thirteen hidden objects: a ladybug, comb, envelope, spinning top, pair of jeans, kite, hourglass, toucan, fish, banana, bird, butterfly, and turtle?

Country Store

You can find any crazy thing at a country store. Can you find the twelve hidden objects: a teacup, watch, hot dog, slipper, pair of glasses, crown, ring, mallet, sock, knife, cupcake, and umbrella?

Broom Hockey

Broom hockey is a fun and inventive game for winter holidays. In this picture find the dog's head, pencil, comb, rose, squirrel, goldfish, postage stamp, spool of thread, golf club, paintbrush, sailboat, bird, coffee mug, and heart.

Angelfish

The angelfish float softly through the water. There are sixteen objects hidden in this undersea world. Can you find the mermaid, apple, bird, shark, bone, button, clover, comb, fried egg, light bulb, lizard, mushroom, seal, shell, snake, and turtle?

Sprucing Up for Spring

When the snow melts and the ground thaws, it's time to plant your garden. There are twenty objects hidden among the busy children. Can you find the ice-cream cone, mouse, crayon, clothespin, trumpet, toothbrush, glove, hammer, clock, paper clip, feather, comb, chicken, candle, teacup, sock, seal, frog, fish, and book?

Summer Vacation

This summer, the Frog and Mouse families vacation at the same pond. Can you find the fifteen objects hidden in this picture: a horse's head, parrot, wishbone, musical note, lizard, exotic bird, mushroom, frying pan, western hat, rocket, sun, pair of pliers, goose's head, loaf of bread, and pocketknife?

Beach Volleyball

The kids love to play volleyball on the hot sand. In this picture are twelve hidden objects: a nail, seashell, paintbrush, flag, penguin, hammer, hat, crayon, banana, trained seal, thumbtack, and rabbit. Can you find them all?

Dream Princess

At night Sally dreams that she is a magic princess in faraway lands. In this picture are fourteen hidden objects: a circus elephant, snake, sailboat, bird, butterfly, hat, flute, oboe, ice skate, rabbit, swan's head, book, clothespin, and banana. How many can you find?

Transportation Museum

With the help of a museum, it's easy and fun to learn about life in the past. In this museum picture there are twenty hidden objects. Can you find a pocket watch, golf club, flag, diamond ring, megaphone, skate, umbrella, sailboat, comb, needle, nail, paintbrush, cowboy boot, ladder, spinning top, envelope, vase, scrub brush, table, and top hat?

Barrel Racer

Tanya and her horse turn sharply around the barrels in the race. Can you find thirteen hidden objects in this picture: a crab, screwdriver, bird, cat, squirrel, alligator, hammer, pair of pliers, fish, ruler, camel, toadstool, and dog's head?

Teddy Bear Picnic

The Bear family always has a good time at a picnic. Can you find the tulip, butterfly, book, teacup, shoe, paintbrush, binoculars, cupcake, slice of pie, pencil, sock, tomahawk, watch, golf club, and ice-cream bar?

Carousel

Cindy, Carl, and their friends love to ride the carousel horses around and around. In this picture are twenty-seven hidden objects: a candy cane, cowboy hat, ski cap, pair of shorts, duck's head, shoe, pair of binoculars, vase, spaceship, swan, mushroom, bottle, comb, banana, button, sombrero, boat, mop, lollipop, spur, penguin, doughnut, little fish, coffeepot, wristwatch, sock, and iron.

Spy School

"First you've gotta get a trench coat and a good hat." Hidden in this picture of spy school are a cat, baseball bat, sewing needle, crayon, piggy bank, nutcracker, ladle, spool of thread, seal, toothbrush, diamond ring, and teacup.

Busy, Busy Elves

The busy elves are busy, busy building a new house. In this picture find the table, witch's head, wooden spoon, dragon's head, music stand, queen, chair, dog, banana, torch, hat, broom, wooden fork, candle, corn on the cob, shoe, worm, brush, bear, water pitcher, strawberry, rowboat, magic lamp, and ax.

Tidepools

There's a whole new world under the water that's fascinating to study. You can study this picture and look for the seventeen hidden objects: a flipper, shovel, pelican, sailboat, shell, angelfish, surfboard, dolphin, sea gull, bucket, pirate's head, duck, sea captain's head, seal, anchor, head of a person wearing a broad-brimmed hat, and lighthouse.

56

Monkey Fun

There's nothing but monkey business here. Can you find the snail, fish, bug, carrot, boomerang, bell, candle, whale, alligator, ring, bone, comb, star, musical note, baseball, bird, toothpaste tube, worm, feather, and saltshaker?

Deserted Mansion

The goblins and ghouls come to this house every night. . . do you dare to find the fourteen hidden objects? Look for an ice-cream soda, cracked egg, diamond ring, crown, letter V, wishbone, dancer, sailboat, spinning top, baseball bat, mushroom, ladder, bunch of grapes, and skier.

Ferdinand, Isabella, Columbus

The king and queen of Spain are delighted when Columbus offers treasures from the New World. In this picture find the ship, squirrel, bird, horse's head, paintbrush, elephant's head, bell, hat, fish, and scissors.

Library

Everyone can find something good to read in the library. In this picture can you find the whale, candle, queen's head, pumpkin, ice skate, high-heeled shoe, king's head, fish, and canoe?

Circus

The excitement of the circus makes everyone smile! You will smile when you find the elephant's head, kite, apple, ice-cream cone, goose's head, bell, baseball, piece of rope, pipe, bone, golf club, baseball bat, T-shirt, pair of pants, and mushroom.

Bighorn Sheep

The bighorn sheep are at home on steep, craggy mountaintops. In this picture look for the teddy bear, ice-cream cone, cardinal, flipper, guitar, spoon, goose, scissors, high-heeled shoe, rabbit, and ax. Did you find them all?

Carolers

"We bring you good tidings for a happy new year!" Make merriment with the carolers by finding the thirteen hidden objects: a cupcake, saw, candy cane, flower, piece of cake, paintbrush, piece of pie, umbrella, cup, spoon, book, carrot, and ice-cream bar.

Croquet Tournament

The mice use grapes for a game of croquet, with the help of some cooperative inchworms. In this picture find fourteen objects: an archery bow, umbrella, cap, jar, duck, seal, butterfly, hat, egg, wooden shoe, sailboat, canoe, telescope, and bird.

John James Audubon

Here Mr. Audubon sketches a bird in its natural habitat. Can you find the nine hidden objects? Look for a paddle, owl, praying mantis, mouse, fish, fox, canoe, eagle's head, and alligator's head.

A Good Day's Catch

Willie and Racer head for home with a surprise for dinner. In this picture find an octopus, kiwi, snake, cat, boot, squirrel, and fish, and the heads of an elephant, fawn, lioness, doe, bear, and eagle.

Baking a Pie

Little Bear tries to get a taste of a fresh berry and honey pie. While the pie cools, look for a cane, skateboard, banana, pie slice, sock, ladder, crown, fork, quarter moon, bumblebee, baseball, star, fish, pair of glasses, horseshoe, key, and candle.

Pintails

As the days turn colder, the pintail ducks fly south to warmer regions. In this picture find the kangaroo, cat, eagle's head, mouse, seal, archery bow, rabbit's head, butterfly, goose, fish, dog's head, sheep's head, banana, bat, and candle.

68

Mr. Scarecrow and His Friends

It looks as though this scarecrow is too friendly to do his job well! Can you find the thirteen hidden objects in this picture? Look for a cat, rabbit, fish, cow's head, horse, man's head, hen, grasshopper, pig, ear of corn, goat's head, snail, and apple.

The Animals' Picnic

When all the flowers blossom in May, the animals have a picnic day. Look for the nineteen hidden objects in this picture: a turtle, ax, ice-cream cone, shark, dog, spoon, sheep's head, broom, safety pin, elf hat, baseball bat, hanger, shoe, teacup, pair of scissors, sock, key, dove, and seal.

Three Men in a Tub

Three men try to sail the ocean in a rub-a-dub tub. In this silly picture find the cat, bird, squirrel, pear, airplane, anchor, pig, sock, and woman's head.

Growing Up

Lucy Ostrich stands on her toes when it's time to measure up! In this picture find the ice-cream cone, paper clip, golf club, boomerang, baseball, baseball bat, banana, crescent moon, dragonfly, two fried eggs and two strips of bacon, triceratops's head, stegosaurus, and cat's head.

Rapunzel

Rapunzel lets down her golden hair to the prince, her true love. Hidden in this picture are twelve objects: a pterodactyl, hammer, rabbit, telephone receiver, spider, cap, tulip, lizard, cardinal, candle, pot, and toothbrush.

Rabbits on the Slopes

It's a great day for skiing, and the slopes are packed! In this picture find the pig, pencil, key, sailboat, book, wool hat, comb, light bulb, shark, toothbrush, pliers, clog, sock, carrot, bird, fan, and squirrel.

74

A Windy Day

It's a windy day on the farm! Can you find the twelve hidden objects before they blow away? Look for a key, bird, leaping deer, resting deer, three decorated eggs, envelope, chicken, lion's head, present, and rabbit.

A Frogtime Band

Fred Frog and his friends try out a tune in the middle of the marsh. While they play, look for a fish, key, bell, needle, penguin, clothespin, bottle, seal, bug, bird, caterpillar, lizard, safety pin, sheep's head, and cat's head.

Country Ride

This wild ride is sure to stir up the countryside! See if you can find the twelve hidden objects before the cats speed away. Look for a toothbrush, rabbit, pizza pie, weasel, pencil, book, hamster's head, moon, spoon, cardinal's head, hot dog, and mouse.

Answers

Front cover

page 3

page 4

page 5

Answers

page 6

page 7

page 8

page 9

Answers

page 10

page 11

page 12

page 13

Answers

page 14

page 15

page 16

page 17

Answers

page 18

page 19

page 20

page 21

Answers

page 22

page 23

page 24

page 25

Answers

page 26

page 27

page 28

page 29

Answers

page 30

page 31

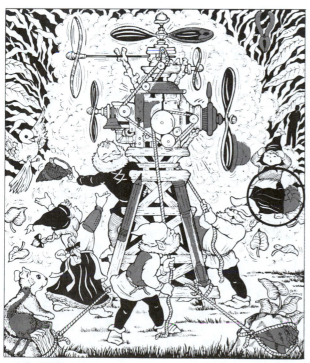

page 32

page 33

Answers

page 34

page 35

page 36

page 37

Answers

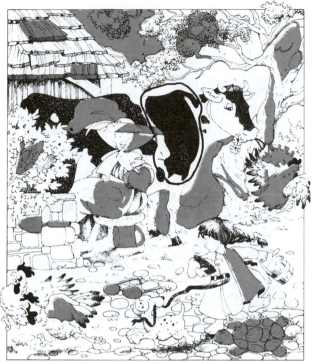

page 38

page 39

page 40

page 41

Answers

page 42

page 43

page 44

page 45

Answers

page 46

page 47

page 48

page 49

Answers

page 50

page 51

page 52

page 53

Answers

page 54

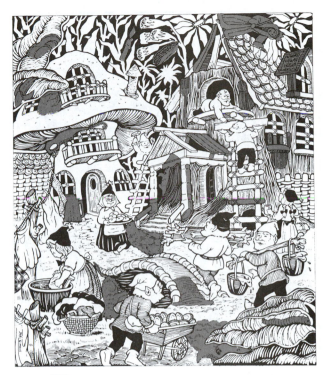

page 55

page 56

page 57

Answers

page 58

page 59

page 60

page 61

Answers

page 62

page 63

page 64

page 65

Answers

page 66

page 67

page 68

page 69

Answers

page 70

page 71

page 72

page 73

Answers

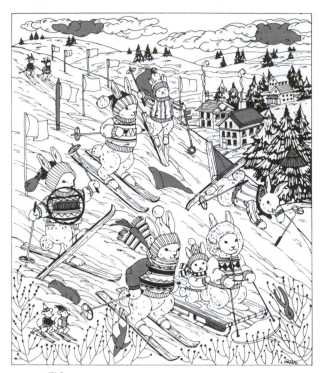

page 74

page 75

page 76

page 77